TCU HORNED FROGS

BY SAM MOUSSAVI

SportsZone
An Imprint of Abdo Publishing
abdopublishing.com

abdopublishing.com

Published by Abdo Publishing, a division of ABDO, PO Box 398166, Minneapolis, Minnesota 55439.

Printed in the United States of America, North Mankato, Minnesota
052018
092018

THIS BOOK CONTAINS RECYCLED MATERIALS

Cover Photo: Andrew Dieb/Icon Sportswire/AP Images
Interior Photos: Andrew Dieb/Icon Sportswire/AP Images, 1; Matthew Visinsky/Icon Sportswire/AP Images, 4–5; Matthew Pearce/Icon Sportswire/AP Images, 6, 9, 43 (bottom); Brandon Wade/AP Images, 10; AP Images, 12–13, 17, 18, 22, 42 (top), 43 (top left); Bettmann/Getty Images, 14; The Sporting News/Getty Images, 20–21, 43 (top right); F. Carter Smith/AP Images, 25; David J. Phillip/AP Images, 26–27, 32; Donna McWilliam/AP Images, 28, 42 (bottom left); John Russell/AP Images, 31; Jae C. Hong/AP Images, 34–35, 42 (bottom right); Michael Prengler/Cal Sport Media/AP Images, 38; Austin Gay/AP Images, 40; Chris Brown/Cal Sports Media/AP Images, 44

Editor: Julie Dick
Series Designer: Craig Hinton

Library of Congress Control Number: 2017962094

Publisher's Cataloging-in-Publication Data

Names: Moussavi, Sam, author.
Title: TCU Horned Frogs / by Sam Moussavi.
Other titles: Texas Christian University Horned Frogs
Description: Minneapolis, Minnesota : Abdo Publishing, 2019. | Series: Inside college football | Includes online resources and index.
Identifiers: ISBN 9781532114618 (lib.bdg.) | ISBN 9781532154447 (ebook)
Subjects: LCSH: American football--Juvenile literature. | College sports--United States--History--Juvenile literature. | Texas Christian University Horned Frogs (Football team)--Juvenile literature. | Football--Records--United States--Juvenile literature.
Classification: DDC 796.332630--dc23

TABLE OF CONTENTS

1 THE HUNT IS ON 4

2 THE LEGACY 12

3 A TOUGH TRANSITION 20

4 THE JOURNEY UPWARD 26

5 PRESENT-DAY PURPLE 34

TIMELINE 42

QUICK STATS 44

QUOTES & ANECDOTES 45

GLOSSARY 46

MORE INFORMATION 47

ONLINE RESOURCES 47

INDEX 48

ABOUT THE AUTHOR 48

Quarterback Trevone Boykin came up big against the Sooners in 2014.

1

THE HUNT IS ON

ON OCTOBER 4, 2014, TEXAS CHRISTIAN UNIVERSITY (TCU) HAD A CHANCE TO MAKE A NAME FOR ITSELF IN THE COLLEGE FOOTBALL WORLD. THE FOURTH-RANKED OKLAHOMA SOONERS HAD ARRIVED AT AMON G. CARTER STADIUM IN FORT WORTH, TEXAS, TO FACE THE TCU HORNED FROGS.

The game would be played in front of a packed crowd dressed in TCU purple. As was often the case, Oklahoma was favored to win. Some even thought that Oklahoma's team was the best in college football that year. But the game would be settled on the field, and the Horned Frogs hoped their home crowd could help put them over the top. It was time for TCU to see where it stood in the Big 12 Conference.

TCU got the ball first. The Horned Frogs had scored on the opening drive of their first three games that season. Oklahoma had not allowed any points on opening drives that year. Something had to give.

B. J. Catalon (23) watches as tight end Cliff Murphy recovers Boykin's fumble for the game's first touchdown.

On the opening drive, the Horned Frogs moved quickly into Oklahoma's red zone, where they faced third-and-goal from the 1-yard line. Quarterback Trevone Boykin kept the ball on a draw play and lunged for the end zone. He took a hard hit just before crossing the goal line. The ball popped out of his arms and rolled into the end zone. But TCU tight end Cliff Murphy recovered the ball for a touchdown. The Horned Frogs had caught a lucky break and took a 7–0 lead.

On TCU's second drive, Boykin completed two long passes to All-American wide receiver Josh Doctson. The Frogs were set up deep in Sooner territory again. Junior running back B. J. Catalon ran the ball untouched into the end zone to finish the drive. That put TCU on top 14–0. Amon G. Carter Stadium rocked as the TCU fans went crazy. This was the moment they had been waiting for. The home team was on its way to beating a mighty opponent with the whole country watching.

But Oklahoma would not go away that easily. The Sooners answered with two quick touchdowns of their own. At halftime the score was tied 24–24. The back-and-forth game promised to have a classic finish.

TCU fans had to relish what was a huge moment for the program. Few people had expected much from the Horned Frogs when they

PAPER CHAMPIONS

The National Collegiate Athletic Association (NCAA) used to decide its Division I national championship on paper, not on the field. Media organizations and coaching associations once conducted polls of their members to determine the national champion. Whichever team got the most votes would be declared the champion by each organization. That often led to split championships when one team didn't win every poll. In 1992 the NCAA began taking steps to ensure that the No. 1 and No. 2 teams would face off in a bowl game to determine the national title on the field. This move eventually resulted in the College Football Playoff, which now slots the top four teams in the country in two national semifinal games played at major bowl sites. The winners then meet in the national title game.

HORNED FROGS

TCU's colors are purple and white, and its mascot is a horned frog—sort of. The animal that represents the teams is actually a horned lizard, a reptile with spiky skin found on TCU's campus. Horned frogs are not native to Texas.

joined the Big 12 in 2012. How could a small private university compete with schools two or three times its size? And indeed, the Horned Frogs had a losing conference record in each of their first two Big 12 seasons.

But by 2014, TCU had earned some respect. The Horned Frogs started the season with easy wins against Samford, Southern Methodist University (SMU), and Minnesota. That put them at No. 25 in the Associated Press (AP) national poll. But they still needed to prove themselves against their toughest conference opponents. Oklahoma provided a convenient measuring stick. In 2012 and 2013, Boykin had played well enough to keep TCU close against the Sooners, but the Horned Frogs lost both games. Could TCU break through against Oklahoma in 2014?

The second half started with a Sooners touchdown that gave Oklahoma its first lead, 31–24. This would usually mark the moment where TCU would begin to stumble and let a tough opponent such as Oklahoma take control of the game. But this Horned Frogs team was different. Less than three minutes later, Boykin answered with a 29-yard touchdown pass to junior receiver Deanté Gray. That tied the score 31–31 heading into the final quarter.

TCU's mascot is named SuperFrog. He's actually a super-sized horned lizard.

TCU needed a big play to get the Sooners on their heels, but its offense had slowed down. The early momentum on that side of the ball had all but disappeared. The home crowd was silent, nervous that Oklahoma would make enough plays to pull out a win, just as it had in years past. So it was up to the TCU defense to swing the game.

Senior linebacker Paul Dawson delivered the much-needed play in the first minute of the fourth quarter. With Oklahoma facing third down near midfield, Sooners quarterback Trevor Knight dropped back to pass. He fired a dart to his right, but he didn't see Dawson, who jumped into the passing lane and made the interception.

Fans stormed the field after TCU defeated the Sooners.

But that wasn't all. Dawson raced 46 yards for a touchdown. Carter Stadium erupted again. Dawson's teammates mobbed him. Everyone clad in purple had to believe *this* could be the moment of breakthrough.

Those thoughts were put on hold, however, when the Sooners blocked the extra-point kick. Even worse, Oklahoma's Zack Sanchez scooped up the ball and brought it back the other way for a rare defensive two-point conversion. Instead of enjoying a seven-point cushion, TCU led by only four, 37–33.

The stadium fell silent. TCU's fans had seen this many times before against a tough opponent. They were prepared for the worst. But this time, TCU did not fold. The defense did not let Oklahoma score another point, snuffing out five Sooners possessions in the fourth quarter. TCU's fans stormed the field after the huge win. Carter Stadium's field was a sea of purple, with fans and players celebrating together. This was the victory the program had craved.

The win propelled TCU to No. 9 in the next national poll. This was TCU's highest ranking since it moved to the Big 12. It also gave the team confidence it could beat any opponent in the nation. One week later, TCU met Baylor in a classic. Baylor was ranked fifth in the nation. The game was a shootout. TCU led 58–37 early in the fourth quarter. But then the unthinkable happened. Baylor scored 24 unanswered points to win 61–58 and ruin the Horned Frogs' perfect record.

Led by Heisman Trophy finalist Boykin, TCU won its final seven games to finish the regular season 11–1. But the loss to Baylor kept TCU out of the new College Football Playoff.

The Horned Frogs were invited to a postseason bowl, though. They faced Mississippi in the Peach Bowl in Atlanta. TCU easily handled Ole Miss 42–3 to cap a 12–1 season. The year ended on a positive note, but it left the Horned Frogs hungry for more.

Though the mission was not complete, 2014 was an enormous year for TCU. A lot of hurdles were crossed, setting the stage for the Horned Frogs to be considered one of the top programs in the nation.

Quarterback Sammy Baugh threw 39 touchdown passes for TCU from 1934–36.

2

THE LEGACY

TODAY THE TEXAS CHRISTIAN UNIVERSITY CAMPUS IS LOCATED IN DOWNTOWN FORT WORTH, TEXAS. THE SCHOOL WAS FOUNDED UNDER A DIFFERENT NAME IN A DIFFERENT CITY. IN 1873 BROTHERS ADDISON AND RANDOLPH CLARK OPENED A NEW SCHOOL IN THORP SPRINGS, TEXAS. THEY CALLED IT THE ADDRAN MALE AND FEMALE COLLEGE. ALMOST 20 YEARS LATER, THE SCHOOL MOVED TO WACO, TEXAS, AND IT ADOPTED ITS CURRENT NAME IN 1902. THE SCHOOL RELOCATED TO FORT WORTH IN 1910 AFTER A FIRE DAMAGED THE BUILDINGS.

The football team began play in 1896. Its first game was a victory over Toby's Business College of Waco. TCU finished its first season with a record of 1–1–1. Joe J. Field, TCU's first coach, led the team to a winning season and its first victory over Texas A&M in 1897. Today's rivalries in the state of Texas grew from early games such as those.

In 1909 TCU joined the Texas Intercollegiate Athletic Association (TIAA). The 1912 squad had its best season to

Baugh was a tremendous quarterback and punter at TCU and in the NFL.

date, finishing with a record of 8–1. Under coach W. L. Driver, the Frogs gained attention in 1920 for winning their first TIAA title. TCU even played in a bowl game that year, back in an era when there weren't many bowl games. The Frogs faced Centre College of Kentucky in the Fort Worth Classic on New Year's Day 1921. Centre College was a short-lived independent power in the early 1920s. The Centre Colonels proved their might with a 63–7 victory over the Horned Frogs.

TCU joined the Southwest Athletic Conference (SWC) in 1923. The SWC was home to powerhouse programs such as Texas, Texas A&M, and Arkansas. The competition rose to a higher level in the new conference. But the Horned Frogs adapted quickly, going 7–1–1 in 1925.

In 1929 Francis Schmidt took over as head coach and led TCU to its first SWC title the same year. The Frogs' 9–0–1 record included wins over in-state rivals Texas A&M, Rice, Texas, and Baylor, plus a tie with SMU. This was the Frogs' first taste of major success, and they went on to win the conference again in 1932.

SLINGIN' SAMMY

Sammy Baugh arrived at TCU in 1933 with plans to play baseball. But football coach Dutch Meyer convinced Baugh to join his team as well. By the end of his sophomore year, Baugh had earned the starting quarterback position. In 1935 he led TCU to its first national championship.

The *Fort Worth Press* nicknamed him "Slingin' Sammy" for his strong and accurate passes. Baugh threw 39 touchdown passes at TCU, but he also starred as a defensive back and punter. Meyer called Baugh "the greatest athlete I ever saw."

After college, Baugh wasn't sure he wanted to play professional football. He spent one year playing minor league baseball but eventually settled in as one of the greatest quarterbacks in National Football League (NFL) history. In his 16-year pro career, he led the NFL in completion percentage eight times, he had the league's best punting average five times, and he intercepted a league-high 11 passes in 1943.

DAVEY O'BRIEN

Davey O'Brien did a little bit of everything on the football field, and he did it all well. In 1938 he became the first TCU player to win the Heisman Trophy as he led the Frogs to the national championship. O'Brien threw at least one touchdown pass in every game that season and led the nation in passing for the second straight year. But he also returned punts and kickoffs, played defense, and was a feared runner as well. Beginning in 1981, the Davey O'Brien Award has been given to the nation's best college quarterback.

Dutch Meyer began his legendary career as head coach in 1934 after Schmidt left to take over at Ohio State. Meyer's time at TCU lasted 19 seasons. He won three SWC championships and led the Horned Frogs to their first two national championships.

The highlight of the 1935 season came in late November when the Frogs hosted the rival SMU Mustangs. The *New York Sun* called it the "Game of the Century." Both teams came in with perfect 10–0 records. The winner would have a great chance to land a coveted invitation to the Rose Bowl. More than 37,000 fans crowded into Carter Stadium, which at the time had a capacity of 30,000.

SMU jumped out to a 14–0 lead. TCU fought back to tie the game in the fourth quarter as All-American quarterback Sammy Baugh connected with Jimmy Lawrence for the tying touchdown. But on the next drive, SMU converted a fourth-down play with a 48-yard touchdown pass to running back Bobby Wilson. The Mustangs held on for a 20–14 victory.

TCU fans were discouraged but not defeated. There was still hope for a special season. Even with the loss, TCU was invited to play in the

Davey O'Brien, *left*, and coach Dutch Meyer watched a game from the sidelines in 1939.

Sugar Bowl on New Year's Day in New Orleans. The game against Louisiana State University (LSU) was memorable more for its miserable weather and strange final score than its exciting plays. Playing through a driving rain on a muddy field at Tulane Stadium, TCU bested LSU 3–2.

The Horned Frogs' 1935 season ended with a 12–1 record. Meanwhile, SMU lost to Stanford in the Rose Bowl, leaving the two Texas rivals with identical records. The right to claim the title of national champions was disputed. Multiple polls named a different champ. However, the Williamson System, which was the only poll taken after the bowl season, named TCU the champion.

TCU halfback Johnny Hall, *in white*, struggled to gain yards in the 1939 Sugar Bowl.

Losses to Texas Tech and Texas A&M ruined any hopes of a repeat championship run in 1936. But the Horned Frogs made history by winning the first Cotton Bowl Classic, beating Marquette 16–6 on New Year's Day 1937 in Dallas.

After a down year in 1937, the Horned Frogs put together the finest season in school history. Quarterback and Heisman Trophy winner Davey O'Brien led TCU to top rankings in the AP polls. The Horned Frogs rolled through the SWC thanks to a defense that allowed an average of 5.5 points per game. TCU didn't trail all season as it stormed to a 10–0 record and another trip to the Sugar Bowl. The Frogs then defeated sixth-ranked Carnegie Mellon 15–7. The 1938 team pulled off the first unbeaten and untied season in school history. They were even declared the national champion in the final AP poll.

Meyer coached for another 14 seasons, but his teams never won more than seven games in a season after that magical 1938 campaign. They appeared in the final AP poll of the season only one more time under Meyer—in 1951, when they finished the year ranked No. 11 in the country.

AMON G. CARTER STADIUM

In 1928 philanthropist Amon G. Carter started a campaign to raise money for a new TCU stadium. Carter Stadium opened in 1930. The impressive, open-air stadium has hosted some of college football's biggest games. It's also known as one of the toughest places to play in all of college football. One of its nicknames is "Hell's Half Acre" because opposing teams find it so hard to win there.

In 1953 assistant coach Abe Martin replaced Meyer, and he coached the Horned Frogs for the next 14 seasons. During that time, the Frogs were solid if not spectacular. TCU went to the Cotton Bowl three times in four seasons starting in 1955. Martin won three SWC titles and went to five bowl games in all. His time at TCU marked the end of a stable period for the program. Tough times were coming and the program would have to weather the storm.

The Horned Frogs' 19-year bowl drought ended when head coach Jim Wacker led them to the 1984 Bluebonnet Bowl.

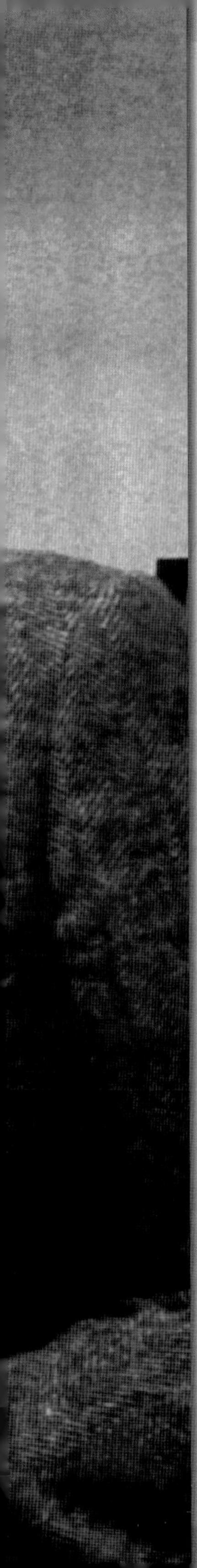

3

A TOUGH TRANSITION

THE TCU FOOTBALL PROGRAM WAS ONE OF THE MOST SUCCESSFUL IN THE COUNTRY. THE HORNED FROGS COMPETED IN ONE OF THE NATION'S BEST COLLEGE FOOTBALL CONFERENCES. GAMES AGAINST THE LIKES OF ARKANSAS, TEXAS, AND TEXAS A&M HELPED TCU GAIN NATIONAL EXPOSURE. THAT HELPED THEM RECRUIT OUTSTANDING PLAYERS FROM ALL OVER THE COUNTRY. FINALLY, THE PROGRAM HAD TASTED POSTSEASON TRIUMPH. TCU HAD ALL THE MAKINGS OF ONE OF THE TOP PROGRAMS IN COLLEGE FOOTBALL.

That all changed dramatically as TCU entered a period of disappointment and adjustment for the program. Abe Martin's retirement in 1966 sent the program reeling. Between 1967 and 1997, TCU went through seven different head coaches and posted a record of 107–225–8 during that time. Unfortunately the struggles did not end on the field. The program had its share of off-the-field woes as well, including a tragedy that shocked the entire college football world.

Head coach Jim Pittman suffered a fatal heart attack during a game.

On October 30, 1971, the Horned Frogs played a road game at Baylor. Shortly after the game began, head coach Jim Pittman suffered a heart attack on the sidelines. The crowd in Waco, Texas, was left stunned as TCU's head coach was rushed to the hospital. His players learned at halftime that the 46-year-old Pittman did not survive.

Pittman was replaced by his top assistant, Billy Tohill, who had arrived with Pittman from Tulane. Though Tohill did a nice job of settling the team, the 32-year-old was not prepared to lead a major college program. After going 5–6 and 3–8 the next two seasons, Tohill was fired. But those seasons looked like TCU's glory days compared with what followed. Jim Shofner went 2–31 in three years as head coach. F. A. Dry arrived from Tulsa but didn't do much better, winning just 12 games in six seasons.

Finally, in 1983, TCU hired Jim Wacker, who had won four Division II national titles at Southwest Texas State and Texas Lutheran. In 1984 the Frogs started the season 8–1 and played in their first bowl game in 19 years. Though they lost in the Bluebonnet Bowl, the season was an encouraging sign that the program was ready to return to greatness under Wacker.

PLAYING THROUGH GRIEF

Jim Pittman arrived at TCU after a successful stint as the head coach at Tulane University. He had a history of heart troubles, but he wouldn't let that keep him from his coaching career. On the night of his fatal heart attack, the Horned Frogs rallied to beat Baylor 34–27. That gave them a share of first place in the SWC. Under interim coach Billy Tohill they won three of their final four games to finish in third place at 6–4–1.

Then trouble came calling again. After the first game of the 1985 season, Wacker learned that some of his players were accepting money and other improper benefits from TCU boosters. This was a violation of NCAA rules. Wacker kicked the offending players off the team and reported the violations to the NCAA. Without several of its key players, TCU won only three games. What had the makings of a dream season turned into a nightmare.

It only became worse in 1986. The NCAA put TCU on probation for three seasons. The penalties included a ban on postseason play and a reduction of the number of scholarships available to the football program. Both penalties severely hampered the ability of Wacker's staff to recruit top players. The Frogs averaged just four wins per season for the next six years.

After he led the Frogs to a 7–4 record in 1991, their first winning season since 1984, Wacker bolted for the head coaching job at the University of Minnesota. Former Heisman Trophy winner Pat Sullivan took over. The highlight of his tenure was a big late-season win at home

GOING WEST

The Southwest Conference fell apart in 1995. Arkansas had already left for the Southeast Conference (SEC) in 1992. Texas and Texas A&M remained the backbone of the SWC, but the promise of big money lured those two programs to the Big 12. There weren't enough teams left to maintain a conference, so the Horned Frogs joined the rest in the search for a new home.

TCU ended up in the Western Athletic Conference (WAC) in 1996. The WAC was traditionally home to smaller universities on the West Coast. But a grand expansion plan nearly doubled the size of the conference, which split into two divisions. The Frogs and their former SEC partners Rice and SMU were part of the Mountain Division. TCU earned its first WAC victory on October 12, 1996, against the University of Texas at El Paso (UTEP). But the Horned Frogs won only five games in their first two seasons in the WAC.

TCU linebacker Gerald Taylor (37) pursues the opposing fullback at the 1984 Bluebonnet Bowl.

over Texas Tech in 1994. The victory pushed the Frogs' record to 7–5 and earned them a bid in the Independence Bowl. But it was all downhill from there for Sullivan, who resigned after going 1–10 in 1997.

But before he left, Sullivan did something that would impact TCU's football program for years to come. He convinced a prep running back from Waco that he should play football at TCU. The young running back was undersized but electric with the ball in his hands. The Horned Frogs' future prospects improved dramatically the day LaDainian Tomlinson set foot on campus.

Coach Dennis Franchione gets drenched by his players after TCU's victory over USC in the 1998 Sun Bowl.

4

THE JOURNEY UPWARD

DENNIS FRANCHIONE, KNOWN AFFECTIONATELY AS "COACH FRAN," BECAME THE HEAD COACH AT TCU IN 1998. THINGS STARTED TO CHANGE FOR THE BETTER IMMEDIATELY UNDER FRANCHIONE. IN HIS FIRST SEASON AS COACH, THE FROGS WENT 7–5 AND WON THE SUN BOWL IN AN UPSET VICTORY OVER THE UNIVERSITY OF SOUTHERN CALIFORNIA (USC). THE 1998 TEAM HAD IMPROVED BY SIX VICTORIES, THE BIGGEST TURNAROUND IN THE COUNTRY THAT SEASON.

The next year, TCU went 8–4 and won a share of the WAC title. LaDainian Tomlinson brought national attention to the program. At 5 feet 10 inches tall, Tomlinson's height was questioned by critics. They did not think a smaller running back could compete at the major college level. But Tomlinson proved the doubters wrong with his speed and heart. Tomlinson finished second in the nation in rushing with 1,974 yards—an average of nearly 168 yards per game. The 1999 team beat East Carolina 28–14 in the Mobile Alabama Bowl.

LaDainian Tomlinson (5) rewrote the record books while at TCU.

An even stronger TCU team opened the new millennium. The Frogs went 10–2 and won the 2000 WAC title outright. Tomlinson was once again impressive. This time he led the nation with an amazing 2,158 rushing yards. At the time, only three other players in NCAA Division I history had rushed for more yards in a season. Tomlinson also scored 22 touchdowns. He earned the Doak Walker Award at the end of the season, given to the nation's top running back.

TCU returned to the Mobile Alabama Bowl, losing to Southern Mississippi, but the season was no failure. The Horned Frogs had been ranked in the AP top 25 for the first time in a decade. They actually cracked the top 10 for the first time since 1959 with a No. 9 ranking before settling in at No. 21 at the end of the season.

Franchione had laid a foundation for success. He had recruited well on both sides of the ball. And he had given his players confidence they could compete with anybody. But he had also gained a national profile due to his success, and that eventually resulted in an offer he found too good to refuse.

TOMLINSON TERRIFIC

LaDainian Tomlinson attended University High in Waco, Texas. He went on to be a superstar during his four seasons at TCU. He finished his Horned Frogs career with 5,387 rushing yards. At the time, only six players had rushed for more career yards in NCAA history. And Tomlinson did the bulk of that work over two seasons. He gained just 538 yards as a freshman and 717 as a sophomore. Then he broke onto the scene as a junior when he rushed for a Division I record 406 yards as well as six touchdowns against UTEP. That record stood until 2014.

In 2000 Tomlinson was a finalist for the Heisman Trophy as he put together one of the most consistently productive seasons in NCAA history. He rushed for at least 119 yards in every game that year. He topped 200 yards in five different games, including 305 more against UTEP, whose defenders must have been glad to see him graduate.

Tomlinson enjoyed a 11-year NFL career, primarily with the San Diego Chargers. He rushed for 13,684 yards and 145 touchdowns in the NFL. He is a member of both the Pro Football and College Football Hall of Fame. TCU retired Tomlinson's No. 5 jersey at a ceremony in November 2005.

Franchione agreed to become the head coach at Alabama just before the Frogs were to play in the 2000 Mobile Alabama Bowl. Defensive coordinator Gary Patterson replaced him as head coach in time to lead the team in Mobile. Continuity in the program allowed the Frogs to recover quickly from Franchione's departure. Patterson's defensive players knew his schemes. The offense would continue running the ball effectively. Something good was happening down in Fort Worth.

TCU switched conferences again in Patterson's first year, this time to Conference USA (C-USA). Patterson believed strong defense was the quickest way to success, so with Tomlinson off to the NFL, the Horned Frogs became more defensive minded. The highlight of 2001 was a 37–22 defeat of Louisville. It was the Cardinals' only conference loss that season. TCU held Louisville's potent offense to eight points below its season average.

CONFERENCE HOPPING

TCU has played in six different conferences. With each move, the team faced an adjustment period. But the Frogs always found their stride pretty quickly. For example, TCU reached a postseason bowl within three seasons of moving to the WAC, C-USA, MWC, and Big 12.

The defense was even better in 2002, holding opponents to only 18 points a game en route to a 10–2 record and a share of the C-USA championship. TCU began to get some national credibility, moving as high as No. 22 in the AP poll. The Frogs won yet another bowl, beating Colorado State in the Liberty Bowl. The trend continued upward in 2003, with the Frogs improving to 7–1 in conference

Jamal Powell (73) and Clif Alexander hoist the Liberty Bowl Trophy after defeating Colorado State 17–3 in 2002.

and 11–2 overall. The program had developed enough consistency to appear regularly in the AP poll. Their next move would put them on the path to even loftier achievements.

At the end of the 2004 season, TCU joined the Mountain West Conference (MWC) in search of better competition. The Horned Frogs wasted no time making their mark on their new conference. They were

TCU kicker Peter LoCoco celebrates the victory over Iowa State in the 2005 Houston Bowl.

picked to finish sixth in the MWC in 2005. Yet they had one of their most impressive seasons. They finished 8–0 in conference and 11–1 overall. The one-two punch of running backs Robert Merrill and Aaron Brown helped the offense average 33 points a game.

The defense was dominant too, once again holding opponents to 18 points a game. Fans filled Carter Stadium for home games. The team claimed its first outright conference title since 1958. TCU capped the magical season with a win over Iowa State in the Houston Bowl. Horned Frogs football was to be taken seriously. TCU finished No. 11 in the AP poll, the program's highest postseason ranking in 46 years.

Over the next three years, the Frogs won a total of 30 games. They finished in the top 10 once and won three bowl games. Patterson had set a standard for the program. His defenses were fast. His offenses used the running game to their advantage. The next step to becoming explosive on offense was to develop a passing attack.

Like Franchione, Patterson made a difference on the recruiting trail. He was able to recruit top players from Texas to come to TCU. He even took some away from state powerhouses Texas and Texas A&M. TCU needed to keep pace with the rest of the nation's top teams. Anything under 10 wins was now unacceptable for the Horned Frogs.

MWC AND THE POWER FIVE

The Atlantic Coast, Big Ten, Big 12, Pac-12, and SEC are considered the "Power Five" conferences in college football. Their schools have a built-in advantage when the postseason schedule is determined. A team that dominates a Power Five conference is viewed as elite and is more likely to earn a spot in the playoffs or at least in one of the top bowl games.

However, the MWC produced some outstanding teams during TCU's years in the conference. Between 2008 and 2011, the MWC placed five teams in the top 10 of the season-ending AP poll.

TCU quarterback Andy Dalton earned the 2011 Rose Bowl Most Valuable Player Award.

5

PRESENT-DAY PURPLE

THE HORNED FROGS REACHED NEW HEIGHTS IN 2009 WITH A 12–0 REGULAR SEASON RECORD, A MOUNTAIN WEST CONFERENCE TITLE, AND THE NO. 3 RANKING IN THE FINAL REGULAR-SEASON AP POLL. THIS WAS TCU'S HIGHEST RANKING SINCE ITS 1938 NATIONAL TITLE. UNFORTUNATELY FOR THE HORNED FROGS, THE SYSTEM USED BY THE NCAA AT THE TIME TO DETERMINE ITS NATIONAL CHAMPION INVOLVED ONLY THE TOP TWO TEAMS. THAT LEFT THE HORNED FROGS ON THE OUTSIDE LOOKING IN. THEY ACCEPTED A BID TO THE FIESTA BOWL, WHERE THEY LOST TO NO. 6 BOISE STATE. BUT THE SEASON STILL PROVED THEY WERE ON THE WAY UP.

The 2010 team followed up with the most successful season in school history. Led by Heisman Trophy candidate Andy Dalton, the team went 8–0 in MWC play. Dalton, a senior quarterback, led a potent air attack that rolled up 541 points, an average of 41.6 per game. That was the fourth-best in the country. The Horned Frogs had the nation's top scoring defense, allowing only 12 points a game.

ANDY DALTON

To say Andy Dalton was a valuable player for TCU would be an understatement. Dalton was the Horned Frogs' starting quarterback from 2007 to 2010. As a freshman, he was named MVP of the Texas Bowl. The next year, he was named MVP of the Poinsettia Bowl. Dalton capped his college football career by earning MVP honors in the Rose Bowl. The title crowned a perfect season for the Horned Frogs. Dalton left Fort Worth as TCU's all-time leader in wins by a quarterback. He was chosen in the second round of the 2011 NFL Draft by the Cincinnati Bengals.

That regular season ended with TCU undefeated and ranked No. 3 again. That meant they just missed a chance to play for the national title. Instead, they settled for beating No. 4 Wisconsin 21–19 in the Rose Bowl on New Year's Day. Dalton, who ran for one touchdown and passed for another, was named the game's Most Valuable Player (MVP).

The 13–0 record was the best mark in TCU history. The Frogs finished the season ranked No. 2 in the final AP poll. They had finally put together an entire season, proving that their recent success was legitimate. And they had achieved success to a degree that TCU supporters had once thought impossible.

The 2011 season wasn't as big a success on the national level, but the Frogs still won their third straight conference title. The offense averaged 41 points a game. But nonconference losses to two old rivals—SMU and Baylor—kept them from the national title's doorstep for a third straight year. TCU ended up 11–2 with a victory over Louisiana Tech in the Poinsettia Bowl and the No. 14 ranking in the final AP poll.

That also was the last year for TCU in the MWC. The Horned Frogs had long been wanting to prove themselves against the best teams. But after the 2011 season, Missouri and Texas A&M left the Big 12 to join the SEC. That created an opening for TCU to join a power conference for the first time. So the Horned Frogs left the Mountain West to become part of the Big 12. Once again it was time for TCU to show the country it could hang in a tough conference. The competition would increase in the Big 12. The coaches and players would need to rise to a new level. But TCU had faced this before.

BCS DRAMA

From 1998 to 2014, the NCAA relied on a system called the Bowl Championship Series (BCS) to determine its national champion. Under the BCS rules, the No. 1 and No. 2 teams in the nation met on the field to decide the winner. This was a big improvement over the former system using multiple polls that often led to a disputed championship. However, the 2009 season demonstrated the flaws built into the BCS.

That year five teams finished the regular season undefeated. Alabama and Texas both went 13–0 and met in the BCS title game. But TCU and Cincinnati both finished 12–0 and were ranked third and fourth, respectively. And Boise State finished 13–0 but ranked sixth. Much of the discrepancy was due to strength of schedule. Alabama (SEC) and Texas (Big 12) faced tougher competition than TCU (MWC), Cincinnati (Big East), and Boise State (WAC).

In 2015 the top four teams had a shot at the title thanks to the new College Football Playoff. Most fans agree it's not a perfect solution but find it preferable to a two-team playoff system.

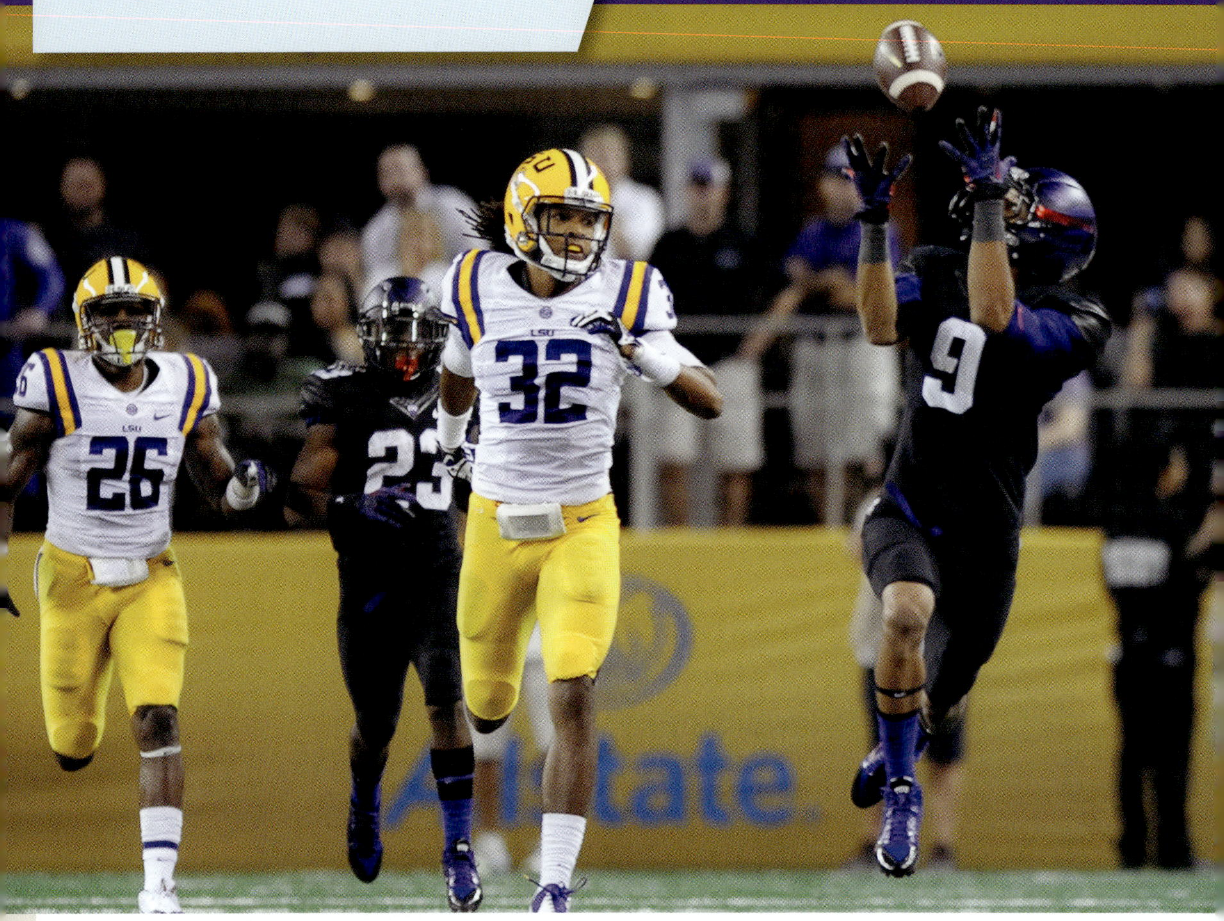

Josh Doctson (9) makes a catch in a 2013 game.

The initial Big 12 season was uneven. Four straight wins earned the Horned Frogs the No. 15 spot in the AP poll, but then they lost five of the next eight games, all against Big 12 teams. Five opponents were ranked in the top 25, including No. 3 Kansas State, which shut down the Frogs 23–10 in Fort Worth. TCU did knock off No. 23 West Virginia and No. 18 Texas, but it was clear the Big 12 was different.

That point was hammered home in 2013. The Frogs limped through a 4–8 season, including a 2–7 mark in the conference. It was TCU's first season without a postseason bowl since 2004. Patterson and his players were determined to make it a one-year absence. The program had worked too hard, and come too far, to fall back.

In 2014 the team had fresh stars on offense in Trevone Boykin and Josh Doctson. Paul Dawson emerged as a leader on the other side of the ball. TCU knocked off three top-10 teams in 2014: Oklahoma, Kansas State, and Ole Miss. These Frogs were well-rounded and explosive. The offense averaged 46 points a game. Boykin emerged as a run-pass threat, while Doctson made countless big catches. Meanwhile the defense allowed only 19 points per game, the eighth-best mark in the country.

The Horned Frogs also learned not to shy away in big moments. In fact, they often stepped up when the lights were brightest. TCU finished 2014 as cochampions of the Big 12. After years of moving to and from lesser conferences, TCU was finally excelling at college football's highest level.

The Horned Frogs began the 2015 season ranked No. 2 in the nation, but it was a far different team that took the field that fall. Even though the Frogs

JOSH DOCTSON

Josh Doctson transferred to TCU in 2012 after playing his freshman year at Wyoming. After sitting out that season due to transfer rules, Doctson went on to rewrite the TCU record books over the next three years. In 2014 Doctson broke TCU's records for receiving yards and touchdown catches in a season. But those marks didn't stand long. Doctson broke his own records during his senior season in 2015, setting the pace with 1,326 receiving yards and 14 touchdown catches. Doctson was selected by Washington in the first round of the 2016 NFL Draft.

TCU quarterback Kenny Hill looks to pass in the 2017 Alamo Bowl.

won their first eight games, they fell three spots in the AP poll over that span because their schedule was relatively weak. Then they stumbled with conference losses at Oklahoma State and Oklahoma, the first two ranked teams they'd faced all year. TCU salvaged its season with a win over No. 7 Baylor and a 47–41 overtime victory over No. 15 Oregon in the Alamo Bowl, earning the No. 7 spot in the final AP poll.

After slipping to 6–7 the next season, the Frogs were back in business in 2017. Senior quarterback Kenny Hill led the way, throwing 23 touchdown passes and only eight interceptions. Though unranked to start the season, TCU climbed all the way up to No. 4 in the AP poll in late October. Two losses to Oklahoma—including one in the Big 12 title game—ruined any national title hopes.

The Horned Frogs capped the year with a thrilling shoot-out against Stanford in the Alamo Bowl in San Antonio. The Cardinal led 31–23 starting the fourth quarter, but a couple of big plays made a huge difference for TCU. First Hill and freshman wide receiver Jalen Reagor connected on a 93-yard touchdown pass. A two-point conversion was unsuccessful, but the TCU defense forced a punt, and senior Desmon White returned it 76 yards for another score and a 36–31 lead. Stanford regained the lead, but TCU kicker Cole Bunce calmly drilled a 33-yard field goal with just over three minutes to play and the Horned Frogs won 39–37. TCU ended up ranked ninth in the final AP poll of the season.

The Frogs' 2017 campaign ended with an 11–3 mark—another double-digit win season, another bowl win, and another top-10 ranking. It was clear TCU had earned its place among the top programs in the country. But staying on top would be another challenge altogether.

TIMELINE

1896
TCU plays its first football game on December 7 against Toby's Business College.

1920
TCU earns its first conference title with a 9–1 season.

1923
TCU joins the Southwest Conference.

1930
TCU defeats Arkansas in the first game in the new Amon G. Carter Stadium on October 11.

1936
TCU defeats LSU 3–2 in the Sugar Bowl on January 1.

1997
LaDainian Tomlinson plays his first game for TCU September 6 against the Kansas Jayhawks.

2000
Gary Patterson takes over as head coach of TCU on December 20.

2001
TCU moves again to Conference USA.

2005
TCU defeats Iowa State in the Houston Bowl on December 31 and goes 11–1 on the season.

2011
TCU defeats Wisconsin in the Rose Bowl to complete a perfect 13–0 season on January 1.

TCU wraps up a 10–0 regular season with a victory against Carnegie Mellon in the Sugar Bowl on January 2.

1939

On November 8, TCU defeats the No. 1 ranked Texas Longhorns 6–0.

1961

TCU coach Jim Pittman suffers a fatal heart attack during a game against Baylor on October 30.

1971

TCU coach Jim Wacker kicks several players off the team for violating NCAA rules. TCU is put on probation.

1985

TCU moves to the Western Athletic Conference.

1996

TCU begins play in the hyper-competitive Big 12 conference.

2012

TCU defeats Oklahoma in a close game on October 4.

2014

TCU routs Texas 50–7 on October 3.

2015

TCU beats Oregon 47–41 in the Alamo Bowl on January 2.

2016

TCU finishes in the top 10 for the third time in four years.

2017

QUICK STATS

PROGRAM INFO*

AddRan Male and Female College, 1896–1901

Texas Christian University, 1902–

NATIONAL CHAMPIONSHIPS

1936

1938

OTHER ACHIEVEMENTS

Conference championships: 18

Bowl record: 16–16–1

KEY PLAYERS

(POSITION, SEASONS WITH TEAM)

Ki Aldrich (C/LB, 1935–38)

Sammy Baugh (QB, 1934–36)

Andy Dalton (QB, 2006–10)

Josh Doctson (WR, 2013–15)

Darrell Lester (C, 1933–35)

Bob Lilly (DT, 1958–60)

Davey O'Brien (QB, 1936–38)

Jim Swink (RB, 1954–56)

LaDainian Tomlinson (RB, 1997–2000)

Greg Townsend (DE, 1981–82)

KEY COACHES

Dutch Meyer (1934–52)
109–79–13; 3–4 (bowl games)

Gary Patterson (2000–)
160–57; 10–6 (bowl games)

Jim Wacker (1983–91)
40–58–2; 0–1 (bowl games)

HOME STADIUM

Amon G. Carter Stadium (1930–)

*statistics through 2017 season

QUOTES & ANECDOTES

Andy Dalton was nicknamed the "Red Rocket" at TCU. Part of his nickname comes from the fact that he has red hair. The other part of it is not so clear. It could stem from his rocket-like throwing arm or his running ability.

TCU's mascot, SuperFrog, is often ranked among the favorite mascots in college football. SuperFrog was created in 1979 by a member of the school's athletic promotions department who wanted to spread "Frog Fever" throughout the campus.

"You don't judge people by how you win, you judge people by how you lose. You get back out, you shake hands. That's the way life is. That's what we do at TCU."—Gary Patterson after a tough loss to Oklahoma in 2017

In 2017 TCU and Texas Tech renewed a tradition by bringing back the Saddle Trophy, which resides with the winner of the most recent Horned Frogs–Red Raiders game. TCU and SMU have a similar tradition with an iron skillet as the trophy.

GLOSSARY

booster
A person or organization that supports an athletic team.

conference
A group of schools that join together to create a league for their sports teams.

draw
An offensive play consisting of a delayed handoff or run by the quarterback.

end zone
The end of a football field where a team tries to score touchdowns.

interception
A pass intended for an offensive player that is caught by a defensive player.

offense
The players on a team who focus on scoring points.

poll
A survey of opinions on a subject, often used to rank college football teams during the season.

postseason
Games played after the regular season ends.

probation
A period when a person or program is closely watched after breaking the rules.

record
The results of the games teams play, consisting of wins, losses, and ties.

red zone
The area of the football field between the opponent's 20-yard line and the end zone.

scholarship
Money awarded to a student to pay for education expenses.

FOR MORE INFORMATION

ONLINE RESOURCES

Booklinks
NONFICTION NETWORK
FREE! ONLINE NONFICTION RESOURCES

To learn more about the TCU Horned Frogs, visit abdobooklinks.com. These links are routinely monitored and updated to provide the most current information available.

BOOKS

Glave, Tom. *Texas Tech Red Raiders.* Minneapolis, MN: Abdo Publishing, 2019.

Myers, Dan. *The Story of the Cotton Bowl.* Minneapolis, MN: Abdo Publishing, 2016.

Wilner, Barry. *Total Football.* Minneapolis, MN: Abdo Publishing, 2017.

PLACES TO VISIT

Amon G. Carter Stadium
2850 Stadium Drive
Fort Worth, Texas 76129
817-257-3764
gofrogs.com/facilities/tcu-facilities-football.html

Amon G. Carter Stadium seats 45,000 people and has been home to the Horned Frogs since 1930. A $164 million renovation of the stadium was completed in 2012. The stadium also hosts the annual Armed Forces Bowl in December.

INDEX

Alamo Bowl, 41

Baugh, Sammy, 15, 16
Bluebonnet Bowl, 23
Boykin, Trevone, 6–8, 11, 39
Brown, Aaron, 32
Bunce, Cole, 41

Carter, Amon G., 19
Catalon, B. J., 7
Clark, Addison, 13
Clark, Randolph, 13
Cotton Bowl Classic, 18, 19

Dalton, Andy, 35
Dawson, Paul, 9–10, 39
Doctson, Josh, 7, 39
Driver, W. L., 14
Dry, F. A., 23

Field, Joe J., 13
Fiesta Bowl, 35
Fort Worth Classic, 14–15
Franchione, Dennis, 27, 29–30, 33

Gray, Deanté, 8

Hill, Kenny, 41
Houston Bowl, 33

Independence Bowl, 25

Knight, Trevor, 9

Lawrence, Jimmy, 16
Liberty Bowl, 30

Martin, Abe, 19, 21
Merrill, Robert, 32
Meyer, Dutch, 15, 16, 19
Mobile Alabama Bowl, 27, 28, 30
Murphy, Cliff, 6

O'Brien, Davey, 16, 18

Patterson, Gary, 30, 33, 39
Pittman, Jim, 22, 23
Poinsettia Bowl, 36

Reagor, Jalen, 41
Rose Bowl, 16–17, 36

Sanchez, Zack, 10
Schmidt, Francis, 15–16
Shofner, Jim, 23
Sugar Bowl, 17, 19
Sullivan, Pat, 24–25
Sun Bowl, 27

Tohill, Billy, 22–23
Tomlinson, LaDainian, 25, 27–28, 29

Wacker, Jim, 23–24
White, Desmon, 41
Wilson, Bobby, 16

ABOUT THE AUTHOR

Sam Moussavi is a novelist and freelance writer based in the San Francisco Bay Area. He has written two sets of young adult novels as well as many nonfiction sports titles.